ADVANCED

MASTER

HANDGUNNING

D1247634

To Marvin, the sharpshooter!

ADVANCED

MASTER

HANDGUNNING

Secrets and Surefire Techniques to Make You a Winner

Charles Stephens

Paladin Press
Boulder, Colorado

Also by Charles Stephens:

Cowboy Action Pistol Shooting: Secrets of Fast and Accurate Gunplay

Cowboy Action Silhouette Rifle: Winning Techniques
for Western Competition

How to Become a Master Handgunner: The Mechanics of X-Count Shooting

Thompson/Center Contender Pistol: How to Tune, Time,
Load, and Shoot for Accuracy

Advanced Master Handgunning:
Secrets and Surefire Techniques to Make You a Winner
by Charles Stephens

Copyright © 1994 by Charles Stephens

ISBN 0-87364-787-4
Printed in the United States of America

Published by Paladin Press, a division of
Paladin Enterprises, Inc.
Gunbarrel Tech Center
7077 Winchester Circle
Boulder, Colorado 80301 USA
+1.303.443.7250

Direct inquiries and/or orders to the above address.

Visit our Web site at www.paladin-press.com

Contents

Technical data presented here, particularly data on the use of and training with firearms, inevitably reflects the author's beliefs and experiences with particular firearms, equipment, components, and techniques under specific circumstances that the reader cannot duplicate exactly. Therefore, the information in this book should be used for guidance only and approached with great caution. Neither the author, publisher, or distributors of this book assume

any responsibility for the use or misuse of information contained in this book. It is presented for information purposes only.

The handgun shooter of today is blessed with having the choice of owning several of the most accurate shooting pistols of the century. Manufacturers of ammunition for these handguns have also made giant strides in the development of fodder with which to feed these ultra-accurate pistols.

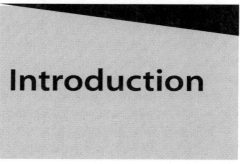

On-site training by masters of the craft of shooting is offered from coast to coast to any and all enthusiasts who wish to pay the fee these experts charge. Books written on the many aspects of handgun shooting occupy the bookshelves of stores and are also available by mail as advertised in many monthly firearm magazines.

Both teachers and books of handgun shooting skills provide the basic and even advanced methods and mechanics of shooting accurately and/or swiftly. Both sources show the handgun student how to master this very important survival skill.

But after the students of these masters leave the instruction sites, they are on their own again! After the students read a book, even though it may be the best tutorial on any given bookstore shelf, he or she is on their own again! They are on their own to pursue the quest of mastering what could be a life-saving survival skill by applying recently acquired knowledge of how to do it.

Advanced Master Handgunning is different from most of the other books written on the subject. As long as it is in the possession of and available to students, they will not be on their own to master the mysteries of accurate shooting.

This tutorial doesn't just provide sound mechanics of accurate shooting to the reader. It also provides the principles of self-teaching methods as applied to the learning and retention of the skills used in shooting a handgun accurately and on demand, as various survival situations may require. Because this book instructs the handgun shooter how to teach himself, the student is never left to the pursuit of this valuable endeavor on his own, without a coach or instructor.

Advanced Master Handgunning also takes the reader beyond the basic mechanics of X-count shooting to a higher level of skill development. This sequel to my first book, *How to Become a Master Handgunner,* includes the advanced mechanics of X-count shooting as applied not only to motionless targets but also to the difficult skills required for shooting moving and long-range targets.

By reading, remembering, and applying the principles of self-teaching methods of shooting both accurate-

Always visually inspect if a handgun is unloaded before handling it further.

ly and on demand, the reader should be able to progress rapidly in his or her pursuit of that seemingly evasive skill known as handgun accuracy. To the best of my knowledge, no other book on the subject of handgun shooting presents such important information in such a clear and concise manner as does this one.

Before continuing with this book, you must understand a few important words of caution. Anytime you handle a firearm, regardless of how familiar you have become with it, always treat it as though it is loaded. Always check a pistol to see if it is unloaded before handling it further. Always point the gun downrange before placing your trigger finger within the trigger guard. Never, but never, point a firearm at another person unless you fully intend to shoot.

CHAPTER ONE

Advanced Master Handgunning presents the principles of self-teaching methods of accurate handgun shooting. It also contains advanced mechanics of shooting not only still targets but moving and long-range targets as well.

Before any handgun user can understand or achieve any success in mastering these advanced skills, he must have mastered basic, accurate shooting techniques. At the least, the novice should be educated in  and possess a sound knowledge of the mechanics of accurate pistol shooting. A summary of these mechanics, which are contained in detail in *How to Become a Master Handgunner*, is presented in this chapter.

THE GRIP

Of all the basic mechanics of accurate handgun shooting, the grip is the most important. A perfect grip on the handgun will enable the pistollero to control the gun and point it in the direction of the target, regardless of the speed required. This grip will also allow the handgunner to shoot a perfect X on the target, be it a paper target at the shooting range or a dangerous criminal intent upon doing harm.

For paper-target shooting, the perfect grip is one in which the weak hand is used to fit the pistol into the strong hand as high up on the grips as possible. The pistol is held using moderate pressure by either or both hands, if regulations allow two-handed shooting.

Moderate pressure is that amount which allows the pistol to be gripped as hard as possible without causing the muzzle to shake.

For all shooting requirements where both hands are available to grip the handgun, the fingers of the strong and weak hands press straight back toward the center of the backstrap using a moderate amount of pressure. The little fingers and the end joints of the thumbs do not apply any pressure to the pistol, nor does any other part of the hand. The heels of the hands touch slightly to the left of the center of the backstrap. Remember, the grip is as high on the gun as possible without allowing the hands to come into contact with the hammer or slide if shooting a slide-operated semiautomatic.

If the grip does not feel comfortable, minor adjustments with the hands on the pistol grip should be made, or custom grips should be fitted to the individual's hands for the type of gun being shot. Once you have developed a comfortable grip well enough to draw, grasp, and shoot the pistol, don't change it again.

Grip the pistol as high on the frame as possible, with the heels of the hand slightly touching to the left of the backstrap.

Fingers of both strong and weak hands press straight back with moderate pressure.

The perfect grip applies sound principles and force vectors. No slick gimmicks or other miracles can allow the handgunner to shoot high X-counts consistently. A solid, comfortable grasp of the pistol while using the fingers as explained above will give the handgunner the opportunity to shoot perfect scores.

TRIGGER PRESS

Almost everyone has heard the term "squeeze the trigger." Don't do it! It is simply impossible for almost anyone to hold and squeeze and hold and squeeze a trigger until the handgun fires with any certainty of hitting the center of the intended target. If you want to hit the target in its X-ring, then you are going to have to *press* the trigger. Pulling and squeezing have absolutely nothing to do with shooting a handgun.

If you play golf or softball or any other game that requires you to swing something, then you can master the basic mechanic of pressing the trigger of a handgun. When you swing a bat or a golf club at a ball, you should begin your swing slowly, then increase the speed as the bat or club continues to approach the ball.

Simply press on the trigger with increasing pressure until the gun fires.

Once the swing of the bat or golf club is speeding toward the ball, the batter or golfer doesn't stop it until after the ball is struck. As he completes his press of the trigger, a handgunner may make slight body-balance movements while manipulating the gun to keep his sights aligned on target, but if he wants to master this basic mechanic of shooting accurately, his trigger press will be continuous, like that of the batter's or golfer's swing, until the gun fires.

This swinging trigger press may be likened to that of pulling a full water bucket up a well casing. You begin to pull slowly on the rope, which is looped over a pulley, then increase your speed using an increasing amount of force downward. This same swinging movement is what the handgunner wants to achieve when he presses the trigger. He simply presses on the trigger with an increasing amount of force until the gun fires!

AIMING THE PISTOL

This swinging type of trigger press is made possible by the handgunner learning how to aim the pistol correctly. Once your sights are aligned, they should be pointed toward the general area of the center of the intended target. Remember this! The aligned sights are not pointed at a tiny, small X in the center of the target. They are pointed at a larger, general area in which the X is located!

This technique is similar to putting a golf ball. The golfer imagines a larger circle surrounding the hole in the green. Aiming near the center of this imaginary circle, the golfer then putts the ball, which travels to the center and drops into the hole!

As a novice shooting enthusiast gains experience while shooting a handgun, the larger general area that contains the X will shrink to a smaller area. As he becomes more proficient at mastering accurate shooting skills, his ability to group several shots in the center of the target will gradually improve.

FOCUS ON THE FRONT SIGHT

You've probably also heard that to shoot a handgun accurately, you must hold the body precisely still while shooting and focus your eyes on the target, not your sights. Bull! No way! A shooter uses a comfortable shooting posture, which he balances like a smooth dancer on the dance floor, while controlling the steadiness of his hold on the pistol as he focuses on the front sight and presses the trigger.

Sound complicated? It is! But like any complicated process, the whole action is broken down into parts. The individual parts in this case are the simple, basic mechanics that are practiced separately and then together until one masters them as a whole. This process is much like learning Morse code or how to type on a typewriter. The student starts off simply and slowly, learning and typing one character at a time. With practice he improves by being able to type a whole word instead of one character at a time. So

Focus on the front sight while pressing the trigger.

don't panic at this stage! Shooting a handgun accurately is just as easily learned as using a typewriter.

Focus on the front sight. Watch the alignment of the rear and front sights out of the corner of your eye while maintaining your focus on the front sight only. Look the focused front sight into the general area of the center of the target while pressing the trigger. Boom! The gun fires, more unexpectedly than actually controlled, and you have an X-ring hit.

You know you are focusing on the front sight when it is clear and sharp in your vision. While shooting at a target on the firing range, if your front sight becomes blurred, stop your shooting process for a moment. Switch your focus to your rear sight until it becomes sharp and clear. Now move your focus back to the front sight. As this sight becomes sharp and clear again, continue with the shooting process.

It is physically impossible to focus on more than one object in more than one focal plane at the same time with the naked eye. You always have a built-in error warning system while shooting. If your front sight is not sharp and clear while you are focusing on it, then you should go see an eye doctor and be fitted with glasses. There are also various di-opter devices on the market that one can attach to the lens of safety glasses to allow you to focus on the front sight of the pistol while maintaining clear vision of the rear sight and the target at the same time!

You control the focus of your eyes. You also control the movement of the pistol when aligning the sights with the intended target. Make subtle but sure movements of the handgun from the side, bottom, or top of the target, then into the general area of the center of the target, while pressing the trigger.

SHOOTING STANCES

To a certain degree you can take the wobble out of the gun, but you can never, and should never, take the wobble out of the body. It is this body wobble, so to speak, that controls proper balance, which allows the handgunner to maintain the degree of steadiness required to enable him to shoot accurately.

The handgunner's stance should be comfortable and allow him to maintain body balance like a smooth dancer. Among the popular shooting stances today are the isosceles, the Weaver, and the one-hand free stance.

The one-hand free stance is just what it says. The stance is the most generally used and accepted by target shooters who shoot while holding the handgun with only the strong hand.

Some people may believe that it is both silly and unwise not to use both hands while shooting. This is almost but not quite true, as somewhere, sometime during your lifetime, you may be confronted with a deadly situation. During this confrontation, you may only have one hand available with which to shoot a hostile person that is endangering your life or the lives of your loved ones.

Although you may never use the one-hand free stance, it is described here so that you can at least try shooting with it. At the least, you will gain some insight into the disadvantages of shooting a handgun while using only one hand. On the other hand, you may want to try shooting from this stance using the strong hand, then using the weak hand so that you become familiar enough with it to gain confidence in your ability to shoot with either hand.

The one-hand free stance is taken by the shooter aligning his feet parallel to the target line. This naturally places his body perpendicular to this same line.

In the one-hand free stance, hook the thumb of the weak hand over your belt.

You will want to be comfortable, so point your toes outward. Hold the gun hand with the pistol against the side of your rib cage while keeping the barrel pointed downrange. Place the other hand about belt high, with the thumb hooked in the belt above the opposite pants pocket (the pocket below the gun hand). If not wearing a belt or pants, simply hold the palm of the free hand against your waist below the gun hand.

Keep your trigger finger out of the trigger guard! With the gun hand and elbow held against your torso, this is called the ready position. Turn your head so that it faces the target squarely. Look at the target with both eyes. Breathe normally! You should be standing quite comfortably, with unrestricted breathing. If not, move your feet and body slightly until you do.

At the command or when ready to fire, bring the gun hand with the pistol down from your torso and point it at the target. Your weight should be distributed evenly between both legs and feet. Your shooting arm will be locked and held straight, pointing at the target. Your knees will be slightly bent; the forward knee will perhaps be bent a little more than the other. Neither knee will appear to be bent to the casual observer, as the legs are still straight, just relaxed at the knees.

Try shooting some dry-fire practice (pistol unloaded) from this stance with either hand. Notice that as you breathe in, the sights raise above target center, and as you exhale, they dip below the center of the target. In order to stop this rising and dipping motion, the handgunner must hold his breath. During this respiratory pause, you press the trigger and fire the pistol. You may want to hold three-quarters, half, or maybe a third lung-full of air when you press the trigger. Whatever condition is comfortable for you is the one to use.

While holding the gun hand in the ready position, close your eyes. That's right, close your eyes. Point your gun at the target, then open your eyes. Where are the sights pointed in relation to either side of the target? If they are not pointed on the target, shift your feet and torso slightly until they are aligned on target.

This is your natural point of aim, where your body is most comfortable standing in relation to the target. Look where your feet are now in relation to where the target is located. Remember to place them in this same position every time you shoot from the one-hand free stance.

Regardless of the minor changes you make to your stance to be comfortable, some of the components should never be altered. One component is the erect head. The head should be held erect, with the eyes looking straight at the target. This head and eye position must be consistent from shot to shot or you will not hit the center of the target each time.

One of the most popular shooting stances while using a two-handed grip on the handgun is the isosceles stance. This stance is assumed by facing the target and spreading your feet a comfortable distance apart. Your feet and body are perpendicular to the target line. Toes are comfortably turned out. Bring the pistol up with the sights aligned on the target. Your elbows should be locked, or almost so. Bend your knees slightly so that your leg muscles feel relaxed. Your head should be held erect, with the eyes looking straight ahead at the target.

When bringing the gun and sights up and pointing the barrel toward the target, don't move the head and eyes to the gun! Once again, close your eyes while pointing the handgun at the target. Open them and make slight feet adjustments that allow the gun to point at the target naturally. Make a mental note of this feet placement for your natural state of pointing the

In the isosceles stance, the shooter's elbows are locked and his knees are bent.

gun at the target while using the isosceles stance. That's all there is to it!

Another popular two-handed stance is called the Weaver stance and its many variations. To assume this stance, face the target and spread your feet comfortably apart. As with the isosceles stance, they should be perpendicular to the target line. Move the right foot back several inches and bring the gun up with the sights aligned on the target. Bend your elbows and bring the pistol in toward your chest a few inches. If you are right-handed, your right elbow will be bent quite a bit more than your left. Both elbows will be pointed toward the ground. Your knees should be locked or almost so, whatever is comfortable for you. Whether your knees are bent or locked, the leg muscles should feel relaxed.

The Weaver stance requires
the shooter to bend his
elbows and lock his knees.

Once more, you must find your natural point of aim
from this stance. When you find it by closing and open-
ing your eyes while pointing the pistol at the target,
note the position of your feet in relation to the target.

Always remember that handgunner shooting
stances were made to accommodate the shooter.
Shooters come in all sizes and shapes. The handgun
enthusiast will adjust his stance to fit his individual
characteristics. Change almost every component of the
various stances except keeping the head erect and the
eyes looking straight at the target and you will still be
correct in your stance.

Experiment for yourself. Cock your head sideways
and look at the target out the corners of your eyes.
Compare your scores shot when doing these things
and see for yourself! You will find that there are com-

Remember! Keep your head erect and look look straight out of your eyes at the target. Call your shot and follow through.

ponents of your shooting stance that you can change that will not affect your ability to hit target center. Then there are those components which should not be changed! Which ones are they? Erect head and face and eyes squared to the target!

SHOT FOLLOW-THROUGH

How do you call your shot and follow through while shooting a handgun? A shooter begins to follow through the moment he raises the pistol and aligns the sights on target. He completes his follow-through when he fires the handgun and calls the shot on target.

He calls his shot by actually seeing the bullet strike the target while looking over the handgun sights.

Like a baseball player swinging a bat, follow-through encompasses the entire process. The batter doesn't wait until the ball reaches the plate to begin his swing. Not unless he wants to strike out, he doesn't! The batter begins his swing as soon as he picks up the ball with his eyes as it leaves the pitcher's hand.

A handgunner who wants to shoot perfect scores doesn't wait until his sights are aligned near target center to begin his trigger pull. His trigger finger touches the trigger and begins the press as soon as the aligned sights approach the outer edge of the target. While the handgunner controls his body balance with minute wobbles to steady the pistol sights and look them onto the near-center area, he is pressing the trigger—slowly at first, then with increasing speed until the pistol fires.

As the gun fires, the shooter continues to look at the target and watches a hole appear in it. This is the process of calling your shot. Completed follow-through allows the shooter to see his hit on the target, provided he is close enough to see the bullet strike it.

The hits in this photo on the right can indicate several possible errors. Among them are 1) the handgunner is not paying enough attention to whether or not his front and rear sights are aligned perfectly; 2) the screws that attach the sights to the pistol that fired these randomly spaced hits are loose and require tightening; 3) the ammunition used to fire these hits is simply very inaccurate for this particular handgun.

You follow through by simply paying attention to what you are doing. It's that simple!

The number-one enemy of the handgunner is letting his mind or attention drift somewhere else while he is shooting. Pay attention and follow through! The end result will be your ability to see and call your shot. You will be successful in hitting the target near center.

This ends the summary of the mechanics of X-count shooting. Use the following diagnostic photographs to evaluate your shooting ability and to help you discover what you may be doing wrong. Correct your problem areas by both dry firing on a blank wall and by actual live-fire practice sessions at the firing range.

No matter how expert a handgunner you may become, always strive to be better. Even when you can make all your shots on demand, press the trigger, and hit the target center exactly when you want to, there is still room for improvement. When you can do these things consistently, it's time to move on to advanced mechanics and shooting moving targets!

The above photo indicates the strong possibility that the handgunner consciously nudged the trigger, called jerking.

This photo indicates that the handgunner may have been heeling the pistol. Heeling is a reaction by the shooter caused by anticipating the gun firing and the impending recoil.

The above photograph indicates that the handgunner may have applied incorrect thumb pressure to the pistol. Remember, the correct grip to use is one where the thumb applies absolutely no pressure to the pistol.

This photograph indicates the handgunner may not have pressed the trigger straight to the rear. He or she has applied trigger finger pressure other than on the line of axis to the bore, resulting in pressure being applied partially to one side of the trigger.

Excel by learning how to teach yourself to shoot perfectly while using self-teaching principles.

CHAPTER TWO

Shooting under the watchful eyes of a coach or instructor, a shooter is shown, step by step, exactly how to shoot correctly (at least as correctly as that particular coach is able to teach another shooter). Once you finish the shooting course and leave, you are on your own again.

Not many shooting instructors teach the handgunner the principles of how to continue teaching himself once he completes the course. One reason, I suppose, is that if the student knows how to teach himself, he will not return for a refresher course, and the coach will eventually run short on students!

Self-Teaching Principles

Knowing the self-teaching principles of any sporting endeavor and applying those principles to your practice regimen is absolutely essential if you are to excel. Shooting master-class scores in competition and being able to hit the vital area of an attacker, on demand and with certainty, demands that you be able to teach yourself during practice sessions.

Make the sporting endeavor easy. Yes! Make it easy for you! This is the first and most important self-teaching principle. By making the process easy, you will give yourself the opportunity to do it perfectly. Make the endeavor difficult and you will most certainly introduce mistakes into the equation, make errors, and learn bad habits.

CLOSE-TARGET DRILLS

How do you make handgunning easy for you?

One way is to make the target larger. Another is to move smaller targets closer. I prefer to use standard-size targets, moving them in closer to me during my practice sessions.

Remember, we want to make the process easier. Making it easier will help us to do it perfectly, or almost so, each time. Moving standard-size targets closer than the regulation distances will enable us to learn the mechanics of shooting correctly. Teach yourself this way and no other. You will learn the mechanics perfectly without introducing mistakes and thus acquiring bad shooting habits.

Move your 50-foot target in to 35 feet. When you can group your shots into the small area of the center, then move the target out to 50 feet and shoot at the regulation distance. Do it this way each time you shoot a practice session. Your scores on targets at regulation distances should improve dramatically by performing this close-target drill at each practice session.

Teach yourself how to find the cause of your errors, then correct your shooting technique. If your hits on the target are not grouped in the center, use the diagnostic photographs in the last chapter to help you discover the problem. Find which of the example targets closely matches yours. It's like correcting your own homework. By doing so, you teach yourself how to correct your missed shots.

If your shots are stringing downward from center toward six to eight o'clock, you are probably jerking the trigger, flinching, or both. Flinching and jerking the trigger are problems that can usually be attributed to a combination of errors in your shooting mechanics. You may be aiming at too small an area or the very point of center on the target. If so, you're trying to be too precise with your aim, introducing a large muzzle shake, then consciously nudging the trigger. Your smooth trigger press becomes a conscious, jerky motion. You thus anticipate the firing of the pistol and the impending recoil. The result is not only the jerking of the trigger but also flinching caused by an opposite and equal reaction to recoil.

Another example of teaching yourself to grade your homework may be analyzing a badly shot target on which the bullet hits are strung out from center toward twelve to two o'clock. These shots may well have been caused by heeling the pistol while shooting.

Heeling is another error in shooting mechanics introduced by the handgunner as a separate reaction from flinching to anticipated recoil. It too may be caused by the shooter trying to be too precise with his aim on too small a point on the target. As a result, the handgunner again nudges the trigger but doesn't jerk it this time. He nudges the trigger just enough to antic-ipate the pistol firing. As a result of this shot anticipa-tion, he pushes at the pistol grip with the heel of his hand, called heeling.

How do you, the handgunner, teach yourself to correct these errors in your shooting mechanics? You move the target in closer and practice shooting it until you once again are doing all the mechanics correctly. Only when your shots are grouping inside a small area of the center do you move the target back out to regu-lation distance.

You, the handgunner, must grade your own work. No one else can do it better than you! Grade your shooting performance by reading your target hits. Use the photographs at the end of Chapter 1 to search for what you may be doing wrong. Go back to the close-target drill and practice until you get it perfect. It's easy to teach yourself! The feedback from doing things the correct way will enable you to progress rapidly with your shooting skills.

Don't try to progress too fast. A handgunner should build a sound, solid foundation of skills by taking it one step at a time. As long as you are consistently shooting target center, you are building your skills at the correct rate of development.

You will develop your ability to shoot with lightning speed while hitting targets at far distances by doing the close-target drills. When you have learned your mechanics of accurate shooting by building up and maintaining a high level of accuracy slowly but positively, you will seldom if ever be affected by match pressure to do well, or any other type of pressure for that matter.

DRY-FIRE PRACTICE

Teach yourself by dry-firing at a wall. While sitting in your favorite living room chair, take your unloaded pistol and point it at a brightly lit blank wall. Align the sights, then with your eyes focused upon the top of the front sight, press the trigger until the hammer falls. What did you see?

Your front sight may be bent or canted ever so slightly to one side. Is it? Is the blueing on the sight marred? If you were actually focused on the front sight and concentrating on sight alignment, you should have noticed the physical peculiarities of your pistol sights.

Try this dry-fire routine again. This time press the trigger faster. Dry-fire five more times, pressing the trigger a little faster each time while watching your front sight. You should eventually reach a trigger-press speed that causes the front sight to dip markedly below the top of the rear notch. This is your trigger press threshold. This threshold determines how quickly you can press the trigger and still shoot precisely and accurately. A handgunner develops this threshold through correct practice.

Use this dry-firing drill to teach yourself how to develop your trigger speed threshold as well as handgun steadiness. The steadier you grip the gun, the steadier the sights will look to your eyes, and the quicker you will be able to press the trigger to its threshold speed.

CHAPTER THREE

The sure ability to hit moving targets with a handgun doesn't require the handgunner to be a magician. Almost anyone can do it. Moving-target shooting ability, however, does require the handgunner to learn some advanced skills with which to perform such feats.

These new, advanced mechanics can be used by the handgunner to continue to develop his ability to shoot motionless targets as well. For the 35 years that I have been involved in competition handgun shooting, I have never quite been able to get even the still targets to sit motionless for me while I am shooting at them!

Advanced Shooting Stances and Mechanics

Impossible, you say. Yes, you're right. Still targets don't move around and dance while waiting for some handgunner to shoot them. It's the handgunner that moves around during his efforts to shoot the target.

We will simply pretend for the moment that the still target is really doing the dancing. Thus we will apply the same advanced mechanics of accurate shooting to these dancing, still targets as we will to actual moving targets. We'll just learn these advanced mechanics while first shooting the dancing, still targets. Sounds confusing, but it really isn't!

THE ADVANCED STANCE

The universally known shooting stances will not be used to shoot moving targets. By restricting the shooter's body movements, they are just too limited when shooting moving targets is required. No stance that restricts the body's ability to balance itself can be used when performing the more difficult sport of shooting at—and hitting with absolute certainty—moving targets.

The new stance is simply called the moving-target stance. It is less rigid than any of the universal stances. It is more comfortable for the shooter to maintain over longer periods of time without becoming fatigued. The moving-target stance also allows complete freedom for the handgunner's mind/body coordination to balance as much as possible in holding the pistol steady enough during complete follow-through of the shooting process.

To assume this new, advanced stance, the hand-

In the moving-target stance, the shooter places more weight on the forward foot.

gunner places his feet almost parallel to the line of movement of a target moving from one side to the other. The same foot placement may also be used to shoot targets that are moving directly away from or toward the handgunner. In these situations, the handgunner's feet will be almost perpendicular to the target's line of movement.

After placing your feet properly in relation to the target's line of movement, place more weight on your forward leg and foot than the other. Do this by leaning into your stance. Remember that the target is moving and may require more than one shot by the handgunner to hit it. It may move left, right, away from or toward you. You simply cannot stand flat-footed and ordinarily expect to get more than one opportunity to shoot at a moving target. If you do not lean into the stance, the recoil of the gun will usually lift the barrel and sights above the target so much that a second shot may not be possible before it moves out of range. Also, by leaning into your stance as you engage a moving target, the body's balance is not upset as much when the gun recoils as it would be if you had stood flat-footed. Thus you can regain your balance more rapidly and bring the gun down for a second shot.

How much should you lean into your stance? There are just too many variables to be more specific, including target speed, height of target above the ground, and the anatomy and strength of the handgunner. You should lean enough to remain comfortable, yet retain your balance. The feet placement and weight shift of this stance are not as rigidly fixed as in the universal handgunner stances. By allowing this freedom of movement, the shooter is allowed to "dance" more comfortably while performing his "trick shots" on moving targets.

Actually, any hit on or near the center of a moving

target is not the result of any magical trick shot. Neither is it the result of an accidental shooting! Such a feat is simply taking the performance of the handgunner to the highest level of this challenging sport. To accomplish this feat requires both correct practice through the application of self-teaching methods and learning these advanced mechanics well enough.

ADVANCED MECHANICS

After placing the feet correctly and shifting your weight more on the forward leg and foot, use the sum of your body-balance movements to raise the pistol sights to the still target that you are practicing on at close range. Do not use individual muscles of the hands or arms to raise the pistol; use only the whole

Shift your weight and lean forward slightly.

or sum of the body-balance movements to do this.

Shift your weight and lean forward slightly until the pistol sights are aligned a couple of inches beneath the target. Now use these same body-balance movements (not just the arms and hands by themselves) to lean slightly backward. This backward movement will raise the pistol and sights to where the shooter wants them, near the general area of the center of the target. I've found that I get better results (more bulls-eye's and Xs) by using this backward shift to raise the sights on target than by firing the pistol at the point where I have lowered them beneath the target center. This is probably due to a small amount of tension that is added to the process as I am raising the pistol. A lot of tension would not be desirable, as it would probably cause the muzzle to wobble. Now touch the trigger gently with your trigger finger.

While you're exhaling some of the air in your lungs, your pistol sights will drop slightly. Gravity will also cause the pistol sights to drop slightly more. At this point in the shooting process, use the sum of your body movements, including a slight backward bending movement, to gently raise the sights enough to compensate for gravity and your respiratory lowering of the sights. While your body is raising the sights the small amount that should be required to bring them to bear on the general area of the near center, press the trigger!

Your pistol fires, hitting the still target as you dance with the sum of your body-balance movements. Watching the target center, you observe a hit. That's all there is to it!

You have just used the moving-target stance along with the other advanced mechanics of accurate shooting to hit a still target. These advanced mechanics were A) using the sum of your body movements rather than hand or arm muscle movement to steady the pistol, and B) using body weight shifting on your forward leg and foot to control the movement of the pistol sights to a point just below the general area of the target center. You simply let your body dance against gravity and your exhaling to do the final movement of the pistol sights.

LONG-RANGE SHOOTING POSITIONS

As with shooting moving targets, the universal standing stances also will not be used while using a handgun for long-range target shooting. Long-range handgunning requires a much more stable platform from which to shoot than the handgunner can obtain from any stance used for standing and shooting. Only two positions—or stances if one wishes to continue using the same terminology—offer the stable platform required. These are the prone and the Creedmore.

The prone position may best be used when speed as well as stability are required and for intermediate long-range handgun shooting. For safety reasons which will be explained later, this position should also be used when the handgunner is firing a revolver or semiautomatic pistol.

To go prone, the handgunner places his pistol in the strong hand, then drops straight down to the ground on his knees. Using the weak hand and the strong hand holding the butt of the handgun to brace the upper torso, lean forward and lie on the ground.

Roll over on your strong side (the strong-hand side) and shift your body so that it makes about a 90-degree angle with the line of sight to the target. Now bring your weak hand over to complete your normal two-handed grip of the pistol. Stick the butt of the pistol into the ground to aid in holding it steady. If the butt is shorter than your hands, then touch the edge of your hands to the ground.

Roll your body halfway over toward the target while aligning the sights and looking them into the general area of the target center. Breathe normally and press the trigger. That's all there is to it.

Make sure your pistol is unloaded while practicing going prone until you are confident in doing it safely. Practice this prone stance on the comfortable carpet of your living room with the unloaded handgun. You will quickly see the superior stableness it offers in steadying the pistol while shooting.

The Creedmore position or stance is used whenever you are not too rushed to assume it. It is also used for shooting extremely long-range targets and while firing solid-breech, single-shot handguns such as Thompson Center's Contender and Remington's XP-100.

To assume the Creedmore position, hold the handgun in your strong hand while sitting on the ground. Face the target directly and lie down on your back. Bring your knees up and place your feet just in front of

Roll over on your strong side in the prone position.

your buttocks. Spread both feet out from your sides a comfortable distance, usually about 3 or 4 inches, and dig your heels into the ground.

Now bring your weak hand up to the side of your head. While raising your head, move the weak hand underneath it. Place the fingers and thumb on the ground for support and lower your head so that the back of it lies on the wrist just above the hand.

Now bring the pistol up with the strong hand and place the barrel against the leg somewhere between the ankle and your knee. For most people, the barrel will probably be placed against the side of the calf. Brace the gun hand against the side of your leg just above your buttock while aligning the sights and looking them into the general area of the near center of the target. Simple, isn't it!

The Creedmore position is not very speedy to assume until one becomes very familiar with doing it. However, it is the most stable of all shooting positions when extremely long-range target shooting is to be attempted. The Creedmore is the last advanced shooting position that will be used while learning the skills of long-range handgunning.

In the Creedmore position, brace the gun hand against the leg.

TRIGGER RELEASE

Is there a better way to press the trigger other than using an increasing amount of pressure by the trigger finger? No. At least there are no ways that I have found that work as well. But there is a new mechanic closely related to trigger press that will make the difference between being a master handgunner and a super handgunner. This advanced mechanic is called trigger release.

Most shooters never give any thought to their trigger release. They just let it take care of itself! If you want to shoot more accurately and faster, then you must learn how to release the trigger properly. The release of the trigger is just as, if not more, important than the trigger press. By mastering this simple but often unheard of mechanic, a shooter adds measurably to his performance with the handgun.

The correct way to release the handgun trigger is to release it the same way that you press it. Press the trigger with an increasing amount of pressure, then release it. Release it slowly at first, then let the trigger finger move forward increasingly faster, using the force of the trigger return spring.

If you perform the trigger release in this manner, you will make more near-center target hits than ever before. You may move into the rare ranks of the super shooter sooner by mastering this simple mechanic than by learning any other advanced shooting mechanic!

Practice proper trigger release by using the methods of self-teaching principles. Dry fire on a blank wall. Of course, make sure, as always, that your handgun is unloaded before you begin practice. Do not start by letting the trigger return with an increasingly faster finger pressure let-off. First, just let the trigger and trigger finger return to the most forward position with a smooth, steady let-off.

Do it this way a dozen or so times at the beginning of each practice session. Then do it the correct way, with an increasing amount of let-off until the trigger has returned all the way forward under the force of the return spring.

SUBCONCIOUS MECHANICS

This method of self-teaching practice—learning it one step at a time, slowly building up this very important and fundamental mechanic of accurate shooting—will develop the skill the proper way. Doing it this way will also allow you to relegate this mechanic to your subconscious!

Advanced mechanics of accurate shooting are designed to take advantage of natural body movements and comfortable posture. By leaving the accomplishment of these mechanics to naturally occurring actions, we hope to remove the possibility of introducing errors to our shooting procedures. Such errors are caused by body actions and movements that are the result of deliberate, conscious, mental thoughts to bring about a controlled movement.

These advanced mechanics of using sum or whole body-balance movements instead of hand or arm movements and proper trigger press release will be learned through self-teaching methods such as close-target and wall dry-firing drills. These mechanics will be developed well enough to require almost no, or very little, conscious thought by the handgunner to bring them about.

A handgunner develops his shooting mechanics through correct practice so that they become subconscious (never unconscious, and certainly not self-conscious) actions. By doing so, he eliminates what is known as "match pressure." The more your mechanics are developed so that they are performed subconsciously rather than by self-conscious directed action, the less chance you have of introducing errors and being affected by match pressure.

The less deliberate the handgunner's actions during the follow-through of the shooting process, the more likely his success in hitting the near center of the target. This is because deliberate, conscious actions require mental thought at the moment of truth to perform them! Conscious actions require more time to perform than do developed subconscious actions.

When a handgunner is steadying his pistol while shooting at a still target, he has a very short time span in which to press the trigger—that is, if he is to press the trigger while holding the pistol steadily enough so that his shot hits near the target center.

When the handgunner is shooting at moving targets, this short time span becomes extremely short! If you are going to press the trigger correctly during these brief time spans, you do not have time to think and deliberate on the necessary actions required to make a successful hit near target center.

Until the handgunner is properly trained and developed in the basic and advanced mechanics of accurate shooting through self-teaching methods, he or she will most likely not achieve much, if any, success at shooting still or moving targets with any confidence. Confidence will come with the development of these mechanics and relegating them to the subconscious. This development must be built up slowly, like learning to type one character at a time before typing a whole word! I stress this because it is absolutely essential and fundamental to be able to perform handgunning feats successfully.

CHAPTER FOUR

In the last chapter you were introduced to the advanced mechanics of accurate shooting. These mechanics were 1) using the sum or whole body movements in controlling body balance, which is used to hold the pistol steadily, 2) using the sum or whole body movements to raise the pistol and its sights slightly to overcome the sight lowering actions of gravity and exhaling, and 3) trigger return.

Also stressed in the last chapter was how essential

Psychology and Mechanics

and fundamentally important it is for the handgunner to build up these advanced skills slowly. Through the one-step-at-a-time method, the student will develop his skills thoroughly enough by relegating them to that area of the brain that performs them subconsciously. We are effectively using psychology to control as many of the mechanics of accurate shooting as we desire.

The subconscious action requires no time-delaying thoughts that deliberate, conscious action requires. Neither does the subconscious leave any action to accident or chance as does the unconscious action!

For example, the subconscious is where we want our trigger-press action to be stored and initiated. With the storing of this vitally important shooting mechanic in the subconscious, we assure ourselves of a near-center hit if we do everything else correctly. By using the subconscious to initiate and complete our trigger press, we can devote our extremely short time span during which our pistol sights are held steadily near target center to consciously focusing on our front sight (or dot if using an optical sighting device).

My dictionary defines subconscious as "being unaware of." In this context, we are unaware of the mental and physical actions required to shoot a handgun accurately and upon demand at the instant the gun fires.

Physical and mental actions are both required in the performance of shooting a handgun. The former is usually directed by the latter. The study of the latter is known as psychology. Psychological or mental action, like physical action, is the result of some stimulus that causes the action or reaction. A stimulus provides the impulse for us to act.

Such a stimulus may be mental or physical. A physical stimulus would be the sting you receive from a bee. The resulting physical action or reaction to this sting might be running away from the bee, in other words, putting some distance between you and the bee for fear of being stung again! A mental stimulus could be a visual input from your eyes seeing a dangerous criminal intent upon doing you harm. Such input stimulates busy-time mental activity! Let's call this mental activity "conscious" because we take time to deliberate or consider all our options before we physically act upon it.

You consciously think about what the criminal is doing and what he might do to you. You also begin to think about what you should do in response to this threat. For the moment, this busy-time mental activity prevents any and all physical activity on your part. Almost, that is. Your heart and pulse begin to race, and your breathing becomes heavier than normal.

You don't take any deliberate physical action during this mental busy time unless you have practiced doing so! Through correct practice to such a stimulus, you will have relegated a planned response into your subconscious. Given the stimulus, you now would not experience physical inactivity—your immediate response would be subconscious. It might be to immediately run away or to draw your gun and shoot the criminal. Of most importance, you would not have to experience mental busy time and give the advantage to the criminal!

As applied to handgun shooting, if you haven't practiced your mechanics correctly and relegated them to your subconscious, the result might be "chicken of the finger." You see the aligned sights on the target, but you can't seem to get the trigger pressed! Another result might be that you hesitate while thinking about what to do and, out of desperation, consciously nudge the trigger. The result is just as bad as the first. You anticipate the gun firing and/or recoil of the pistol, and the shot does not hit near center.

Subconscious! Once and for all let's clear up the mystique associated with this word. If doing something consciously requires conscious, deliberate attention, then doing it subconsciously requires no deliberate or conscious attention.

A subconscious action or reaction can be compared to an instinctive one. My dictionary defines instinct as "a natural reaction or tendency." A natural tendency is one that is not forced. With our knowledge of applied psychology of shooting mechanics—that is, the study of the mental actions required to perform the mechanics of accurate handgun shooting—and by using our self-teaching principles in practice sessions, we are going to commit to our subconscious the physical and mental actions required to perform these mechanics. By doing so, we will perform these mechanics instinctively. They will become natural reactions! We will not be consciously aware that they are happening.

For a subconscious action to be developed, one must perform it correctly so many times, through repetition, that the channels of communication in the brain that coordinate physical and mental actions required for such performance become clear and distinct. These channels of communication are developed so well that they require no busy time to perform the complex coordinated responses.

This is the secret to the mystique of the subconscious. The channels of communication between all the various parts of the brain are developed so well that the response by the handgunner becomes natural. Nothing is forced!

Develop these channels well through your new self-teaching principles. How well you develop them is limited only by the number of repetitions that you perform.

The handgunning student will only be able to commit the mechanics of accurate shooting to his subconscious by slow repetition of the mental and physical actions involved. There is no other way! If you want to build up your handgun shooting ability and progress from being a master to the rare status of a super shooter, you will do it only through lots of work.

If becoming a super handgunner is for you, then the work required will be fun. The best handgunners in the world enjoy what they do! The many repetitions of the mechanics during devoted practice time, as well as seeing the successful results, is immensely satisfying to such handgunners.

Being able to hit the near center of still targets requires a certain amount of practice. Being able to do it consistently requires even more. For the handgunning student to shoot at and score near-center hits on a moving target requires much more time on the practice range. You either want to learn and enjoy this fascinating sport of moving-target shooting or you don't. It's that simple!

CHAPTER FIVE

The ability to shoot moving targets may be important to the handgunning student for several reasons. One reason may simply be for the challenge that such a sport offers. Another may well be that if the student should ever be confronted by a threat that is not motionless, he will have confidence to take the shot quickly and on demand. He will not freeze during the moment of truth and become just another victim of the criminal.

Shooting Moving Targets

I began shooting moving targets quite casually, mind you. With no intention of ever entering any competition that would require me to be proficient in such skills, one day I simply had an opportunity to have some fun while plinking with one of my favorite pistols.

With my cloned half Ruger Blackhawk, half Ruger Bisley, I took an empty 3-pound coffee can out of the back of my old pickup truck and rolled it down a gently sloping hillside. Aligning the sights of my 7 1/2-inch .357 Magnum barrel on the leading edge of the can, I pressed the trigger.

The resulting impact of the 140-grain hollowpoint bullet on the coffee can caused it to become airborne. As the can hit the ground, I aligned my sights the same as before and pressed the trigger again. The result was the same. It caused an immediate rush of adrenaline to my brain! To put it simply, I hadn't had that much fun shooting since I was a kid doing the same thing to a small pet milk can using an old .22LR rifle.

I had also accidently discovered how to do something that would be immensely valuable to me whenever I was to be shooting moving targets again. When you shoot stationary targets you aim your pistol somewhere near the center area of the target. This will not work on moving targets, unless of course they are very large or close to you.

When shooting moving targets even as large as a coffee can and at distances of 25 feet, the handgunner

Aim at the leading edge of a moving target.

must aim at the leading edge of the target if he is to have any consistent success. Also, follow-through must include bending the whole body in the same direction that the target is moving. You must continue that body-bending movement until after the can is hit.

I find that as long as I apply the advanced mechanic of accurate shooting (where I continue to look my sights into the aiming area while I press and release the trigger correctly) while I continue my body movement in the same direction of target movement, the result will be a good score on the target. Correctly releasing the trigger helps me to complete my follow-through on moving targets!

Do not make a mistake when shooting moving targets and fail to use the self-teaching methods used for shooting still targets. These methods also help to develop your ability to hit moving targets consistently.

You may want to begin like I did—just for the fun of it! Save your old coffee cans for use in practice. If there are no safe hillsides available for you to do your coffee can practice, then simply lay them on the ground about 15 feet away. When you shoot one this close, you are almost guaranteed of instantly having a moving target available for your second shot!

One bit of caution before you start slinging a lot of lead up into the sky. So far all your shooting may have been done correctly, with an earthen berm behind the targets to stop the bullets from going off and hitting something you didn't intend to. Unless you do your shooting very far from the nearest house, human being, or domestic animals like cattle, it is very dangerous to shoot your pistol into the blue sky! I advise against doing so altogether.

Do any moving-target practice with shot-shell loads. Unless you hand-load your cartridges, probably the best way to learn this exciting new sport is by shooting a .22LR pistol loaded only with the small shot shells. Later on you can progress to the larger caliber handguns and use shot shells with these also.

As you develop your ability to hit larger cans, replace them with smaller ones. When you can hit the smaller ones, try some clay targets that shotgun-shooting enthusiasts use for practice. They can be bought at some large discount stores for just a few dollars.

Shooting flying clay targets with a pistol is one of the most challenging sports that I have ever participated in. Even though the practice sessions go faster if you have a partner to take turns throwing the targets and shooting them, it isn't absolutely necessary. To make this sport even more challenging, try throwing the clay targets up with your weak hand and then shooting them while holding the pistol in your strong hand! Reverse the procedure and shoot with the weak hand only.

When your practice and training results in even an

Shooting flying clay pigeons is a great challenge.

occasional hit with the weak hand, your confidence in your shooting ability will reach an all-time high. You will know that should you ever be faced with danger and forced to shoot with either hand, you will have a good possibility of hitting your target.

After you have enjoyed the entertaining rewards of shooting moving targets with shot shells, you may want to develop your skill and confidence by shooting with your favorite defense handgun. There are shooting clubs in most areas that hold action shooting matches. Some of these clubs have a moving target range where the competitors fire at a moving paper target. These moving target ranges have berms behind the target line, where the bullets fired will be stopped safely.

Should you want to participate in such moving-target matches, you will already have learned the skills required to hit the paper target with bullets if you can consistently hit coffee cans or clay targets while using

Use the advanced shooting stance when shooting at moving targets.

the shot shells. Hitting the moving paper targets may actually be easier for you than the cans and clays.

Whether shooting with bullets or shot, remember to use the advanced shooting stance similar to the shotgunning stance. Use your self-teaching principle of close-target drills, or use large targets at first. Only after you have developed your ability to hit these easy targets should you try shooting at more difficult ones.

Keep your practice simple and easy while developing your skills properly. Do it the hard way and you will most certainly introduce errors and develop bad habits that will be difficult to correct.

CHAPTER SIX

What exactly constitutes a long distance over which a handgunner may shoot and hit a target? By my experiences from participating in several types of handgun competitions over many years, I've concluded that any distance beyond 35 yards requires long-range target shooting stances or positions if one is to have any certainty of hitting the target consistently.

Long-Range Target Shooting

Targets located at the closer distances of between 35 and 100 yards are within what I call intermediate long range. These targets can be hit readily by the handgunner who uses revolvers and semiautomatic pistols and who has mastered the mechanics of accurate shooting.

The handgunner will want to do his shooting from the prone position when targets are located at these intermediate long-range distances. The prone position is preferred because it offers the handgunner the necessary stability, and the position can be assumed quickly when speed is of importance.

Handgun shooting at targets located at intermediate long-range distances requires more time for the shooter to secure accurate hits than does close-range handgunning. The shooter needs this extra time to check the alignment of his sights on the target. He will have to give more attention to this aspect of shooting than when firing at targets positioned at close range—that is, if he wants to achieve excellent results.

Other than using the prone position and paying more attention to sight alignment than before, that's all there is to shooting very good scores on targets located at the intermediate long-range distances. The handgunner makes use of the same shooting mechanics required for accurate placement of his shots on close targets. The same self-teaching principles used while practicing close-target shooting are applied to intermediate long-range practice.

Extremely long-range pistol shooting absolutely requires the handgunner to use the Creedmore position if he wants to succeed in hitting the target consistently. Extremely long-range as defined for handgun shooting are distances beyond 100 yards.

Why is the Creedmore position required for these distances? Because it is the most stable from which the handgunner can shoot a pistol. If you want to be assured of hitting a long-distance target with any measure of success, then you must be able to hold the handgun sights steadily on the target while you press the trigger.

At these extremely long ranges, your handgun sights are going to drift and wobble around your tar-

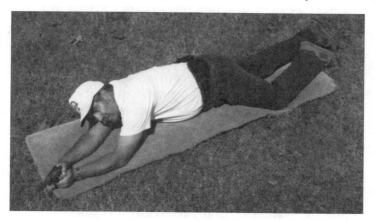

Use the prone position for intermediate long-range target shooting.

get a great deal more than when they did while shooting intermediate- and close-range targets. The less stable a position you shoot from, the more time it is going to take to check your sight alignment and press the trigger until the pistol fires.

Admittedly, the Creedmore position may not seem to be the most comfortable shooting position at first. Any new shooting position requires the handgunner to become very familiar with it while practicing before achieving the confidence necessary to be successful while using it. The Creedmore position is no exception. You will have to do a lot of shooting while using it before you become both comfortable and confident.

A few words of caution before doing any shooting from the Creedmore position. Don't use it when shooting a revolver or a semiautomatic. Hot gasses and lead spitting from cylinder gap and blowback can cause pain and injury to anyone who uses this position.

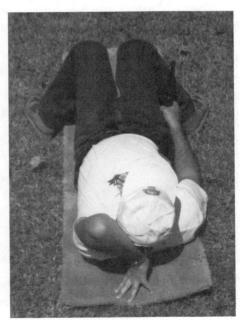

The Creedmore position may not seem comfortable at first.

Normal clothing does not protect the handgunner's legs enough from these hot gasses and lead spitting. Competition shooters who use this position while firing such guns use very thick leather chaps and shields to protect them from injury.

It is generally not unsafe for the handgunner to wear normal clothing while using the Creedmore position to shoot solid-breach single-shot, or repeating pistols. If you were to fire enough shots from these specialty pistols to heat up the barrel, I suppose you could receive a burn or at the least feel a bit uncomfortable as the hot barrel makes contact with the pants leg.

Extremely long-range handgun shooting is made to order for specialty handguns such as the single-shot solid-breach Thompson/Center Contender and the bolt-action Remington XP-100 and 100R. Similar versions of custom-made handguns are also very well-suited to this task.

These long-range handguns perform so well at extremely long-distance shooting primarily because of

Use a protective skirt or chaps when shooting a revolver or semiautomatic pistol from the Creedmore position.

their having been chambered for popular rifle cartridges. Bullets available for these rifle cartridges have very high ballistic coefficients compared to the low coefficients for most handgun-designed bullets.

Seldom does one have the opportunity to make extremely long-distance shots with the handgun without at least some crosswind blowing at the same time he desires to shoot. This is when ballistic coefficients come into play. The higher the ballistic coefficient of a bullet, the less it will be deflected by a crosswind during its travel from the barrel to the target. For example, take a factory-loaded .357 Magnum round fired over a distance of 200 yards from a revolver. If it encounters a 10 mph crosswind and the handgunner does not compensate for drift, the bullet can hit as much as 21 inches to the left or right of the intended target. If that same handgunner was using a Contender chambered for the venerable Winchester .30-30 rifle round in the same 10 mph crosswind, the bullet would only be deflected 6 inches!

Which handgun in the above example would you rather be shooting if you encountered a survival threat? Me too! Revolvers and semiautomatics are fun to shoot and have their applications, but they have their limitations too.

The trouble with crosswinds blowing across your line of fire at extremely long distances is that they are not usually very consistent over short periods of time. If you have the time to wait out the gusty winds, and you have lots of experience in doping constant winds, then you have a better certainty of hitting your target if you are firing a specialty handgun chambered for one of the rifle cartridges.

Once a handgunner develops his extremely long-range target shooting ability, then it will be possible for him to be able to make consistent hits on targets at the close end of the extreme distances using almost any handgun/cartridge combination that has been proven to be accurate enough at that distance. For example, at the 1993 Coors Schuetzenfest competition pistol match, in which the targets were placed at 190 yards (10 yards short of stated regulation), I used a pistol chambered for the little .22LR cartridge. In a wildly blowing crosswind one morning, I fired a single-target score of 236/250. Only one shot of ten drifted out of the bullseye, and that one was only a quarter-inch out.

In the above example, I did use a specialty handgun—a Contender sporting a custom 15-inch Bullberry Barrel Works match-grade stainless barrel. Even though I had such a fine handgun, plus a 12X Leupold rifle scope with a German 3-post crosshair, the job that I was confronted with was simply one of doping the wind correctly. I was pleased with the result!

I also have a very good friend who lives in that notorious Old West town of Tombstone, Arizona, home of the OK Corral. This friend uses an old single-action revolver to do mostof his handgun shooting. He has used this revolver while consistently shooting targets at distances of 50 yards out to 200 yards from the standing isosceles stance! My friend has also won two of the last three annual long-range pistol silhouette matches held nearby. These pistol matches were shot at the same distances of intermediate to extremely long ranges. Admittedly, the Major is one of the best at what he does!

You can also be the best at shooting handguns at extremely long ranges. The same mechanics of accurate pistol shooting at intermediate long ranges are applied, along with practicing and developing your shooting skills by using the principles of self-teaching. Because of the longer distances, eye coordination and checking the alignment of the sights during the longer time that is required to get the trigger pressed are absolutely essential for good scores.

It isn't necessary to have a custom or specialty handgun to be successful at hitting your targets at extreme ranges. Nor is it necessary to own one of those fancy handguns in order to have fun and enjoy the sport of long-range handgun shooting. Just ask Major!

If the conditions or particular threat situation does rear its ugly head, though, use of one of the specialty handguns does measurably increase your chances of survival. I own, practice with, and shoot all of the popular types of handguns, and at all of the possible target distances. You should too!

ABOUT THE AUTHOR

An expert on handgun accuracy, master handgunner and national champion Charles (Charlie) Stephens reveals secret, little-known self-teaching handgun shooting methods to all pistol shooting enthusiasts in his two books, *How to Become a Master Handgunner*, and *Advanced Master Handgunning*. The author resides in Oklahoma and New Mexico, where he continues to write books on gunlore and compete in handgun shooting competitions held throughout the United States.